Ministry to the Sick

Ministry to the Sick

Church House Publishing

Published by   Church House Publishing
Church House
Great Smith Street
London SW1P 3NZ

Copyright ©   *The Archbishops' Council 2000*

First published 2000

0 7151 2035 2

Printed and bound by ArklePrint Ltd, Northampton
on 80 gsm Dutchman Ivory

Typeset in Gill Sans
by John Morgan and Shirley Thompson/Omnific
Designed by Derek Birdsall RDI

The material in this booklet is extracted from *Common Worship: Pastoral Services*. It comprises:

¶   Ministry to the Sick;
¶   Emergency Baptism;
¶   Ministry at the Time of Death;
¶   Bible Readings and Psalms;
¶   Prayers for Protection and Peace.

For other material, page references to *Common Worship: Pastoral Services* are supplied.

Pagination   This booklet has two sets of page numbers. The outer numbers are the booklet's own page numbers, while the inner numbers near the centre of most pages refer to the equivalent pages in *Common Worship: Pastoral Services*.

Contents

The Minister should refer to Common Worship: Pastoral Services *and, in particular, to the Introduction (pages 3–6) and the Theological Introduction to Wholeness and Healing (pages 9–11). For the Celebration of Holy Communion, the president should refer to the complete provisions in* Common Worship: Services and Prayers for the Church of England.

The Celebration of
Holy Communion
at Home or in Hospital

with the Sick and Housebound

Note

Forms of service for a celebration of Holy Communion may be modified or shortened in the light of pastoral need and of the context within which they are used. Any material from authorized rites (such as forms of confession and absolution) may be used. When the Holy Communion is celebrated in the presence of the sick an authorized Eucharistic Prayer, the Breaking of the Bread and the Lord's Prayer are always included.

For further Notes, see page 23.

¶ *Two sample services follow, using Order One (pages 3–11) and Order One in Traditional Language (pages 13–22).*

¶ *If Order Two is used, the service follows the pattern in* Common Worship: Services and Prayers for the Church of England, *pages 228–266.*

The Celebration of Holy Communion at Home or in Hospital

with the Sick and Housebound

Order One

¶ *The Gathering*

The Greeting

Peace to this house and to all who live in it.

(or)

The peace of the Lord be always with you.

Prayer of Preparation

This prayer may be said

All **Almighty God,**
to whom all hearts are open,
all desires known,
and from whom no secrets are hidden:
cleanse the thoughts of our hearts
by the inspiration of your Holy Spirit,
that we may perfectly love you,
and worthily magnify your holy name;
through Christ our Lord.
Amen.

Prayers of Penitence

This or another invitation to confession may be used

[Come to me, all who labour and are heavy laden,
and I will give you rest.]

God shows his love for us
in that while we were still sinners, Christ died for us.
Let us then show our love for him
by confessing our sins in penitence and faith.

This or another authorized Confession is used

All **Almighty God, our heavenly Father,
we have sinned against you
and against our neighbour
in thought and word and deed,
through negligence, through weakness,
through our own deliberate fault.
We are truly sorry
and repent of all our sins.
For the sake of your Son Jesus Christ,
who died for us,
forgive us all that is past,
and grant that we may serve you in newness of life
to the glory of your name.
Amen.**

The president says

Almighty God,
who forgives all who truly repent,
have mercy upon *you*,
pardon and deliver *you* from all *your* sins,
confirm and strengthen *you* in all goodness,
and keep *you* in life eternal;
through Jesus Christ our Lord.

All **Amen.**

The Collect

The president introduces a period of silent prayer with the words 'Let us pray' or a more specific bidding.

The Collect is said, and all respond

All　**Amen.**

¶　# The Liturgy of the Word

Readings

Either one or two readings from Scripture are used.

The Gospel reading follows.

Prayers of Intercession

Appropriate intercessions may be made.

The Laying on of Hands with Prayer and Anointing may follow (pages 42–43).

The Peace

If this greeting has not already been used, the president may introduce the Peace with a suitable sentence, and then says

The peace of the Lord be always with you

All **and also with you.**

These words may be added

Let us offer one another a sign of peace.

All may exchange a sign of peace.

Preparation of the Table

Taking of the Bread and Wine

The table is prepared and bread and wine are placed upon it.

At the preparation of the table this or another suitable prayer may be said

Pour upon the poverty of our love
and the weakness of our praise
the transforming fire of your presence.

All **Amen.**

The president takes the bread and wine.

The Eucharistic Prayer

This or another authorized Eucharistic Prayer is used.

Prayer E

The president says

The Lord be with you   *(or)*   The Lord is here.
All   **and also with you.**   **His Spirit is with us.**

Lift up your hearts.
All   **We lift them to the Lord.**

Let us give thanks to the Lord our God.
All   **It is right to give thanks and praise.**

It is right to give you thanks
in sickness and in health,
in suffering and in joy,
through Christ our Saviour and Redeemer,
who as the Good Samaritan
tends the wounds of body and spirit.
He stands by us and pours out for our healing
the oil of consolation and the wine of renewed hope,
turning the darkness of our pain
into the dawning light of his kingdom.
And so we join with saints and angels
for ever praising you and *saying*:

All   **Holy, holy, holy Lord,**
God of power and might,
heaven and earth are full of your glory.
Hosanna in the highest.
[Blessed is he who comes in the name of the Lord.
Hosanna in the highest.]

We praise and bless you, loving Father,
through Jesus Christ, our Lord;
and as we obey his command,
send your Holy Spirit,
that broken bread and wine outpoured
may be for us the body and blood of your dear Son.

On the night before he died he had supper with his friends
and, taking bread, he praised you.
He broke the bread, gave it to them and said:
Take, eat; this is my body which is given for you;
do this in remembrance of me.

When supper was ended he took the cup of wine.
Again he praised you, gave it to them and said:
Drink this, all of you;
this is my blood of the new covenant,
which is shed for you and for many for the forgiveness of sins.
Do this, as often as you drink it, in remembrance of me.

So, Father, we remember all that Jesus did,
in him we plead with confidence his sacrifice
    made once for all upon the cross.

Bringing before you the bread of life and cup of salvation,
we proclaim his death and resurrection
until he comes in glory.

[Great is the mystery of faith:]
All   **Christ has died:**
Christ is risen:
Christ will come again.

Lord of all life,
help us to work together for that day
when your kingdom comes
and justice and mercy will be seen in all the earth.

Look with favour on your people,
gather us in your loving arms
and bring us with [N and] all the saints
to feast at your table in heaven.

Through Christ, and with Christ, and in Christ,
in the unity of the Holy Spirit,
all honour and glory are yours, O loving Father,
for ever and ever.
All   **Amen.**

The Lord's Prayer

As our Saviour taught us, so we pray

All   **Our Father in heaven,**
hallowed be your name,
your kingdom come,
your will be done,
on earth as in heaven.
Give us today our daily bread.
Forgive us our sins
as we forgive those who sin against us.
Lead us not into temptation
but deliver us from evil.
For the kingdom, the power,
and the glory are yours
now and for ever.
Amen.

(or)

Let us pray with confidence as our Saviour has taught us

All   **Our Father, who art in heaven,**
hallowed be thy name;
thy kingdom come;
thy will be done;
on earth as it is in heaven.
Give us this day our daily bread.
And forgive us our trespasses,
as we forgive those who trespass against us.
And lead us not into temptation;
but deliver us from evil.
For thine is the kingdom,
the power and the glory,
for ever and ever.
Amen.

Breaking of the Bread

The president breaks the consecrated bread.

The Agnus Dei may be used as the bread is broken.

Giving of Communion

The president says this or another invitation to communion

Jesus is the Lamb of God
who takes away the sin of the world.
Blessed are those who are called to his supper.

All **Lord, I am not worthy to receive you,
but only say the word, and I shall be healed.**

This prayer may be said before the distribution

All **We do not presume
to come to this your table, merciful Lord,
trusting in our own righteousness,
but in your manifold and great mercies.
We are not worthy
so much as to gather up the crumbs under your table.
But you are the same Lord
whose nature is always to have mercy.
Grant us, therefore, gracious Lord,
so to eat the flesh of your dear Son Jesus Christ
and to drink his blood,
that our sinful bodies may be made clean by his body
and our souls washed through his most precious blood,
and that we may evermore dwell in him and he in us.
Amen.**

The president and people receive communion.

Authorized words of distribution are used and the communicant replies

Amen.

Prayer after Communion

Silence is kept.

The Post Communion or the following prayer, or another suitable prayer, is said

All   Almighty God,
we thank you for feeding us
with the body and blood of your Son Jesus Christ.
Through him we offer you our souls and bodies
to be a living sacrifice.
Strengthen us
in the power of your Spirit
to live and work
to your praise and glory.
Amen.

¶ Conclusion

The president may use a suitable blessing, or

The peace of God,
which passes all understanding,
keep your hearts and minds
in the knowledge and love of God,
and of his Son Jesus Christ our Lord;
and the blessing of God almighty,
the Father, the Son, and the Holy Spirit,
be among you and remain with you always.

All   Amen.

The Celebration of Holy Communion at Home or in Hospital

with the Sick and Housebound

Order One *in Traditional Language*

¶ *The Gathering*

The Greeting

Peace to this house and to all who live in it.

(or)

The peace of the Lord be always with you.

Prayer of Preparation

This prayer may be said

All **Almighty God,**
unto whom all hearts be open,
all desires known,
and from whom no secrets are hid:
cleanse the thoughts of our hearts
by the inspiration of thy Holy Spirit,
that we may perfectly love thee,
and worthily magnify thy holy name;
through Christ our Lord.
Amen.

Prayers of Penitence

This or another invitation to confession may be used

[Come to me, all who labour and are heavy laden,
and I will give you rest.]

God shows his love for us
in that while we were still sinners, Christ died for us.
Let us then show our love for him
by confessing our sins in penitence and faith.

The following or another authorized confession is used

All   **Almighty God, our heavenly Father,
we have sinned against thee
and against our neighbour,
in thought and word and deed,
through negligence, through weakness,
through our own deliberate fault.
We are heartily sorry
and repent of all our sins.
For the sake of thy Son Jesus Christ,
who died for us,
forgive us all that is past,
and grant that we may serve thee in newness of life
to the glory of thy name.
Amen.**

The president says

Almighty God,
who forgives all who truly repent,
have mercy upon *you,*
pardon and deliver *you* from all *your* sins,
confirm and strengthen *you* in all goodness,
and keep *you* in life eternal;
through Jesus Christ our Lord.

All   **Amen.**

The Collect

The president introduces a period of silent prayer with the words 'Let us pray' or a more specific bidding.

The Collect is said, and all respond

All   **Amen.**

¶ *The Liturgy of the Word*

Readings

Either one or two readings from Scripture are used.

The Gospel reading follows.

Prayers of Intercession

Appropriate intercessions may be made.

The Laying on of Hands with Prayer and Anointing may follow (pages 42–43).

The Peace

If this greeting has not already been used, the president may introduce the Peace with a suitable sentence, and then says

The peace of the Lord be always with you

All   **and with thy spirit.**

These words may be added

Let us offer one another a sign of peace.

All may exchange a sign of peace.

Preparation of the Table

Taking of the Bread and Wine

The table is prepared and bread and wine are placed upon it.

At the preparation of the table this or another suitable prayer may be said

Pour upon the poverty of our love
and the weakness of our praise
the transforming fire of thy presence.

All   **Amen.**

The president takes the bread and wine.

The Eucharistic Prayer

Prayer C

	The Lord be with you.	*(or)*	The Lord is here.
All	**And with thy spirit.**		**His Spirit is with us.**

Lift up your hearts.
All   We lift them up unto the Lord.

Let us give thanks unto the Lord our God.
All   It is meet and right so to do.

It is very meet, right and our bounden duty,
that we should at all times and in all places give thanks unto thee,
O Lord, holy Father,
almighty, everlasting God,
through Jesus Christ thine only Son our Lord.

This or another Short Proper Preface may be used

And now we give thee thanks
that thou hast shown the greatness of thy love for us
by sending him to share our human nature
and accomplish our forgiveness.
He embraces us in our weakness,
he suffers with the sick and the rejected,
and, bringing thy healing to the world,
he rescues us from every evil.

Therefore with angels and archangels,
and with all the company of heaven,
we laud and magnify thy glorious name,
evermore praising thee and *saying*:

All   Holy, holy, holy, Lord God of hosts,
heaven and earth are full of thy glory.
Glory be to thee, O Lord most high.
[Blessed is he that cometh in the name of the Lord.
Hosanna in the highest.]

All glory be to thee,
almighty God, our heavenly Father,
who, of thy tender mercy,
didst give thine only Son Jesus Christ
to suffer death upon the cross for our redemption;
who made there,
by his one oblation of himself once offered,
a full, perfect and sufficient sacrifice, oblation and satisfaction
    for the sins of the whole world;
and did institute,
and in his holy gospel command us to continue,
a perpetual memory of that his precious death,
until his coming again.

Hear us, O merciful Father, we most humbly beseech thee,
and grant that, by the power of thy Holy Spirit,
we receiving these thy creatures of bread and wine,
according to thy Son our Saviour Jesus Christ's holy institution,
in remembrance of his death and passion,
may be partakers of his most blessed body and blood;

who, in the same night that he was betrayed, took bread;
and when he had given thanks to thee,
he broke it and gave it to his disciples, saying:
Take, eat; this is my body which is given for you;
do this in remembrance of me.

Likewise after supper he took the cup;
and when he had given thanks to thee, he gave it to them, saying:
Drink ye all of this;
for this is my blood of the new covenant,
which is shed for you and for many for the forgiveness of sins.
Do this, as oft as ye shall drink it,
in remembrance of me.

One of the following may be used

[Great is the mystery of faith:]

All   **Christ has died:**
Christ is risen:
Christ will come again.

(or)

[Jesus Christ is Lord:]

All   **O Saviour of the world,**
who by thy cross and precious blood hast redeemed us,
save us, and help us, we humbly beseech thee, O Lord.

Wherefore, O Lord and heavenly Father,
we thy humble servants,
having in remembrance
the precious death and passion of thy dear Son,
his mighty resurrection and glorious ascension,
entirely desire thy fatherly goodness
mercifully to accept this our sacrifice of praise
     and thanksgiving;
most humbly beseeching thee to grant that
by the merits and death of thy Son Jesus Christ,
and through faith in his blood,
we and all thy whole church may obtain remission of our sins,
and all other benefits of his passion.
And although we be unworthy, through our manifold sins,
to offer unto thee any sacrifice,
yet we beseech thee
to accept this our bounden duty and service,
not weighing our merits, but pardoning our offences;
and to grant that all we, who are partakers of this holy communion,
may be fulfilled with thy grace and heavenly benediction;

through Jesus Christ our Lord,
by whom, and with whom, and in whom,
in the unity of the Holy Spirit,
all honour and glory be unto thee,
O Father almighty,
world without end.

All   **Amen.**

The Lord's Prayer

Let us pray with confidence as our Saviour has taught us

All **Our Father, who art in heaven,**
hallowed be thy name;
thy kingdom come;
thy will be done;
on earth as it is in heaven.
Give us this day our daily bread.
And forgive us our trespasses,
as we forgive those who trespass against us.
And lead us not into temptation;
but deliver us from evil.
For thine is the kingdom,
the power and the glory,
for ever and ever.
Amen.

(or)

As our Saviour taught us, so we pray

All **Our Father in heaven,**
hallowed be your name,
your kingdom come,
your will be done,
on earth as in heaven.
Give us today our daily bread.
Forgive us our sins
as we forgive those who sin against us.
Lead us not into temptation
but deliver us from evil.
For the kingdom, the power,
and the glory are yours
now and for ever.
Amen.

Breaking of the Bread

The president breaks the consecrated bread.

The Agnus Dei may be used as the bread is broken.

Giving of Communion

The president says this or another invitation to communion

Jesus is the Lamb of God
who takes away the sin of the world.
Blessed are those who are called to his supper.

All **Lord, I am not worthy that thou shouldest come
under my roof,
but speak the word only, and my soul shall be healed.**

This prayer may be said before the distribution

All **We do not presume
to come to this thy table, O merciful Lord,
trusting in our own righteousness,
but in thy manifold and great mercies.
We are not worthy
so much as to gather up the crumbs under thy table.
But thou art the same Lord
whose nature is always to have mercy.
Grant us, therefore, gracious Lord,
so to eat the flesh of thy dear Son Jesus Christ
and to drink his blood,
that our sinful bodies may be made clean by his body
and our souls washed through his most precious blood,
and that we may evermore dwell in him and he in us.
Amen.**

The president and people receive communion.

Authorized words of distribution are used and the communicant replies

Amen.

Silence is kept.

*The Post Communion or the following prayer, or another
suitable prayer, is said*

All **Almighty God,
we thank thee for feeding us
with the body and blood of thy Son Jesus Christ.
Through him we offer thee our souls and bodies
to be a living sacrifice.
Strengthen us
in the power of thy Spirit
to live and work
to thy praise and glory.
Amen.**

¶ *Conclusion*

The president may use a suitable blessing, or

The peace of God,
which passes all understanding,
keep your hearts and minds
in the knowledge and love of God,
and of his Son Jesus Christ our Lord;
and the blessing of God almighty,
the Father, the Son, and the Holy Spirit,
be among you and remain with you always.

All **Amen.**

Notes to the Celebration of Holy Communion at Home or in Hospital

with the Sick and Housebound

1 Prayers of Penitence

These may be omitted when the service has been preceded by a penitential rite.

2 Seasonal Material

Seasonal or Sunday provision may be used in place of that provided here. At Christmas, Easter and Pentecost some at least of the seasonal provision for the Festival should be used.

3 Laying on of Hands and Anointing

The form on pages 42–43 may be used at the Prayers/Prayers of Intercession (Order One) or between the Absolution and Comfortable Words (Order Two).

4 Anointing

Canon B 37 provides that the priest should use 'pure oil consecrated by the bishop of the diocese or otherwise by the priest himself' and that the anointing should be made on the forehead with the sign of the cross. In some circumstances it may also be appropriate to anoint on the hands.

5 Reception of the Consecrated Bread and Wine

Communion should normally be received in both kinds separately, but where necessary may be received in one kind, whether of bread or, where the communicant cannot receive solid food, wine.

6 Spiritual Communion

Believers who cannot physically receive the sacrament are to be assured that they are partakers by faith of the body and blood of Christ and of the benefits he conveys to us by them.

7 Residential Homes

These forms may be used in residential homes where pastorally appropriate.

The Distribution of
Holy Communion
at Home or in Hospital

to the Sick and Housebound

An Outline Order (Order One)

For Notes, see pages 28–29.

The Greeting

This may be

> Peace to this house and to all who live in it.

Words of Introduction

These or other suitable words may be used

> The Church of God, of which we are members, has taken bread
> and wine and given thanks over them according to our Lord's
> command. These holy gifts are now offered to us that, with
> faith and thanksgiving, we may share in the communion of the
> body and blood of Christ.

[Prayer of Preparation]

Prayers of Penitence

These may include this invitation to confession

> [Come to me, all who labour and are heavy laden,
> and I will give you rest.]

> God shows his love for us
> in that when we were still sinners, Christ died for us.
> Let us then show our love for him
> by confessing our sins in penitence and faith.

The Collect

Reading(s) and Prayers

[Laying on of Hands and Anointing]

The Lord's Prayer

Invitation to Communion

[Prayer of Humble Access]

Giving of Communion

Prayer after Communion

This may include the following varied form

All **Almighty God,**
we thank you for feeding us
with the body and blood of your Son Jesus Christ.
Through him we offer you our souls and bodies
to be a living sacrifice.
Strengthen us
in the power of your Spirit
to live and work
to your praise and glory.
Amen.

The Grace *or* a Blessing

The Distribution of
Holy Communion
at Home or in Hospital
to the Sick and Housebound

An Outline Order (Order Two)

For Notes, see pages 28–29.

The Greeting

This may be

> Peace be to this house, and to all that dwell in it.

Words of Introduction

These or other suitable words may be used

> The Church of God, of which we are members, has taken bread
> and wine and given thanks over them according to our Lord's
> command. These holy gifts are now offered to us that, with faith
> and thanksgiving, we may share in the communion of the body
> and blood of Christ.

[Prayer of Preparation]

The Collect

Reading(s) and Prayers

Prayers of Penitence

These may include this invitation to confession

> [Come unto me, all that travail and are heavy laden,
> and I will refresh you.]

> God shows his love for us
> in that when we were still sinners, Christ died for us.
> Let us then show our love for him
> by confessing our sins in penitence and faith.

[Laying on of Hands and Anointing]

[Prayer of Humble Access]

Invitation to Communion

Giving of Communion

The Lord's Prayer

Prayer after Communion

This may include the following varied form

All **Almighty God,
we thank thee for feeding us
with the body and blood of thy Son Jesus Christ.
Through him we offer thee our souls and bodies
to be a living sacrifice.
Strengthen us
in the power of thy Spirit
to live and work
to thy praise and glory.
Amen.**

The Grace *or* a Blessing

Notes to the Distribution of Holy Communion at Home or in Hospital

to the Sick and Housebound

1 **The Distribution of Communion to the Sick and Housebound**

¶ Ministers may be either ordained or lay persons authorized by the bishop to assist in the distribution of Holy Communion.

¶ When the consecrated bread and wine are to be conveyed directly from a celebration to those not present, they are given to the ministers at the distribution or at the end of the service. The ministers may receive communion either at the celebration or with those to whom they take the elements, or on both occasions.

¶ When Holy Communion is distributed at other times to those absent from a celebration, the minister may receive with them but need not do so.

¶ Words of introduction linking the consecrated elements with the celebration at which they were consecrated must be used.

2 **Prayers of Penitence**

These may be omitted when the service has been preceded by a penitential rite.

3 **Seasonal Material**

Seasonal or Sunday provision may be used in place of that provided here. At Christmas, Easter and Pentecost some at least of the seasonal provision for the Festival should be used.

4 **Laying on of Hands and Anointing**

The form on pages 42–43 may be used at the Prayers/Prayers of Intercession (Order One) or between the Absolution and Comfortable Words (Order Two).

5   Anointing

Canon B 37 provides that the priest should use 'pure oil consecrated by the bishop of the diocese or otherwise by the priest himself' and that the anointing should be made on the forehead with the sign of the cross. In some circumstances it may also be appropriate to anoint on the hands.

6   Reception of the Consecrated Bread and Wine

Communion should normally be received in both kinds separately, but where necessary may be received in one kind, whether of bread or, where the communicant cannot receive solid food, wine.

7   Spiritual Communion

Believers who cannot physically receive the sacrament are to be assured that they are partakers by faith of the body and blood of Christ and of the benefits he conveys to us by them.

8   Residential Homes

These forms may be used in residential homes where pastorally appropriate.

The Distribution of Holy Communion at Home or in Hospital

to the Sick and Housebound

A Sample Service (Order One)

This form of service follows the Outline Order on pages 24–25.

For Notes, see pages 28–29.

The Greeting

Peace to this house and to all who live in it.

(or)

The peace of the Lord be always with you.

Words of Introduction

These or other suitable words may be used

The Church of God, of which we are members, has taken bread
and wine and given thanks over them according to our Lord's
command. These holy gifts are now offered to us that, with faith
and thanksgiving, we may share in the communion of the body
and blood of Christ.

Prayer of Preparation

This prayer may be said

All   **Almighty God,**
to whom all hearts are open,
all desires known,
and from whom no secrets are hidden:
cleanse the thoughts of our hearts
by the inspiration of your Holy Spirit,
that we may perfectly love you,
and worthily magnify your holy name;
through Christ our Lord.
Amen.

Prayers of Penitence

This or another invitation to confession may be used

[Come to me, all who labour and are heavy laden,
and I will give you rest.]

God shows his love for us
in that while we were still sinners, Christ died for us.
Let us then show our love for him
by confessing our sins in penitence and faith.

This or another authorized confession is used

All   **Almighty God, our heavenly Father,
we have sinned against you
and against our neighbour
in thought and word and deed,
through negligence, through weakness,
through our own deliberate fault.
We are truly sorry
and repent of all our sins.
For the sake of your Son Jesus Christ,
who died for us,
forgive us all that is past,
and grant that we may serve you in newness of life
to the glory of your name.
Amen.**

The minister says

Almighty God,
who forgives all who truly repent,
have mercy upon *us*,
pardon and deliver *us* from all *our* sins,
confirm and strengthen *us* in all goodness,
and keep *us* in life eternal;
through Jesus Christ our Lord.

All   **Amen.**

The Collect

*The minister introduces a period of silent prayer with the words
'Let us pray' or a more specific bidding.*

The Collect is said, and all respond

All   **Amen.**

Reading(s) and Prayers

Either one or two readings from Scripture are read.

The Gospel reading follows.

Appropriate intercessions may be made.

*The Laying on of Hands with Prayer and Anointing may follow
(pages 42–43).*

The Lord's Prayer

As our Saviour taught us, so we pray

All   **Our Father in heaven,
hallowed be your name,
your kingdom come,
your will be done,
on earth as in heaven.
Give us today our daily bread.
Forgive us our sins
as we forgive those who sin against us.
Lead us not into temptation
but deliver us from evil.
For the kingdom, the power,
and the glory are yours
now and for ever.
Amen.**

(or)

Let us pray with confidence as our Saviour has taught us

All   **Our Father, who art in heaven,
hallowed be thy name;
thy kingdom come;
thy will be done;
on earth as it is in heaven.
Give us this day our daily bread.
And forgive us our trespasses,
as we forgive those who trespass against us.
And lead us not into temptation;
but deliver us from evil.
For thine is the kingdom,
the power and the glory,
for ever and ever.
Amen.**

Giving of Communion

The minister says this or another invitation to communion

Jesus is the Lamb of God
who takes away the sin of the world.
Blessed are those who are called to his supper.

All **Lord, I am not worthy to receive you,
but only say the word, and I shall be healed.**

This prayer may be said before the distribution

All **We do not presume
to come to this your table, merciful Lord,
trusting in our own righteousness,
but in your manifold and great mercies.
We are not worthy
so much as to gather up the crumbs under your table.
But you are the same Lord
whose nature is always to have mercy.
Grant us, therefore, gracious Lord,
so to eat the flesh of your dear Son Jesus Christ
and to drink his blood,
that our sinful bodies may be made clean by his body
and our souls washed through his most precious blood,
and that we may evermore dwell in him and he in us.
Amen.**

The minister and people receive communion.

Authorized words of distribution are used and the communicant replies

Amen.

All   **Almighty God,**
      we thank you for feeding us
      with the body and blood of your Son Jesus Christ.
      Through him we offer you our souls and bodies
      to be a living sacrifice.
      Strengthen us
      in the power of your Spirit
      to live and work
      to your praise and glory.
      Amen.

Conclusion

The minister says the Grace or a suitable blessing.

The Distribution of Holy Communion at Home or in Hospital

to the Sick and Housebound

A Sample Service (Order Two)

This form of service follows the Outline Order on pages 26–27.

For Notes, see pages 28–29.

The Greeting

Peace be to this house, and to all that dwell in it.

(or)

The peace of the Lord be always with you.

Words of Introduction

These or other suitable words may be used

The Church of God, of which we are members, has taken bread
and wine and given thanks over them according to our Lord's
command. These holy gifts are now offered to us that, with faith
and thanksgiving, we may share in the communion of the body
and blood of Christ.

Prayer of Preparation

This prayer may be said

Almighty God,
unto whom all hearts be open,
all desires known,
and from whom no secrets are hid:
cleanse the thoughts of our hearts
by the inspiration of thy Holy Spirit,
that we may perfectly love thee,
and worthily magnify thy holy name;
through Christ our Lord.

All **Amen.**

Our Lord Jesus Christ said:
Hear, O Israel, the Lord our God is one Lord;
and thou shalt love the Lord thy God with all thy heart,
and with all thy soul, and with all thy mind,
and with all thy strength.
This is the first commandment.

And the second is like, namely this:
Thou shalt love thy neighbour as thyself.
There is none other commandment greater than these.
On these two commandments hang all the law
    and the prophets.

All **Lord, have mercy upon us,
and write all these thy laws in our hearts, we beseech thee.**

The Collect

The minister says the Collect.

Reading(s) and Prayers

Either one or two readings from Scripture are used.

The Gospel reading follows.

Appropriate intercessions may be made.

Invitation to Confession

This or another invitation to confession may be used

[Come unto me, all that travail and are heavy laden,
and I will refresh you.]

God shows his love for us
in that while we were still sinners, Christ died for us.
Let us then show our love for him
by confessing our sins in penitence and faith.

All   **Almighty God,**
Father of our Lord Jesus Christ,
maker of all things, judge of all men:
we acknowledge and bewail our manifold sins
    and wickedness,
which we, from time to time,
    most grievously have committed,
by thought, word and deed,
against thy divine majesty,
provoking most justly thy wrath and indignation against us.
We do earnestly repent,
and are heartily sorry for these our misdoings;
the remembrance of them is grievous unto us;
the burden of them is intolerable.
Have mercy upon us,
have mercy upon us, most merciful Father;
for thy Son our Lord Jesus Christ's sake,
forgive us all that is past;
and grant that we may ever hereafter
serve and please thee in newness of life,
to the honour and glory of thy name;
through Jesus Christ our Lord.
Amen.

The minister says

Almighty God, our heavenly Father,
who of his great mercy
hath promised forgiveness of sins
to all them that with hearty repentance and true faith
    turn unto him:
have mercy upon *us*;
pardon and deliver *us* from all *our* sins;
confirm and strengthen *us* in all goodness;
and bring *us* to everlasting life;
through Jesus Christ our Lord.

All   **Amen.**

The Laying on of Hands with Prayer and Anointing may follow
(pages 42–43).

The Comfortable Words

Hear what comfortable words our Saviour Christ saith
unto all that truly turn to him:

Come unto me, all that travail and are heavy laden,
and I will refresh you. *Matthew 11.28*

So God loved the world, that he gave his only-begotten Son,
to the end that all that believe in him should not perish,
but have everlasting life. *John 3.16*

Hear also what Saint Paul saith:
This is a true saying, and worthy of all men to be received,
that Christ Jesus came into the world to save sinners. *1 Timothy 1.15*

Hear also what Saint John saith:
If any man sin, we have an advocate with the Father,
Jesus Christ the righteous;
and he is the propitiation for our sins. *1 John 2.1*

Prayer of Humble Access

This prayer may be said

We do not presume
to come to this thy table, O merciful Lord,
trusting in our own righteousness,
but in thy manifold and great mercies.
We are not worthy
so much as to gather up the crumbs under thy table.
But thou art the same Lord,
whose property is always to have mercy:
grant us therefore, gracious Lord,
so to eat the flesh of thy dear Son Jesus Christ,
and to drink his blood,
that our sinful bodies may be made clean by his body,
and our souls washed through his most precious blood,
and that we may evermore dwell in him,
and he in us.

All **Amen.**

Giving of Communion

The minister and people receive communion. To each is said

The body of our Lord Jesus Christ, which was given for thee,
preserve thy body and soul unto everlasting life.
Take and eat this in remembrance that Christ died for thee,
and feed on him in thy heart by faith with thanksgiving.

The blood of our Lord Jesus Christ, which was shed for thee,
preserve thy body and soul unto everlasting life.
Drink this in remembrance that Christ's blood was shed for thee,
     and be thankful.

The Lord's Prayer

As our Saviour Christ hath commanded and taught us,
we are bold to say

All   **Our Father, which art in heaven,**
hallowed be thy name;
thy kingdom come;
thy will be done,
in earth as it is in heaven.
Give us this day our daily bread.
And forgive us our trespasses,
as we forgive them that trespass against us.
And lead us not into temptation;
but deliver us from evil.
For thine is the kingdom,
the power and the glory,
for ever and ever.
Amen.

Prayer after Communion

All   **Almighty God,
we thank thee for feeding us
with the body and blood of thy Son Jesus Christ.
Through him we offer thee our souls and bodies
to be a living sacrifice.
Strengthen us
in the power of thy Spirit
to live and work
to thy praise and glory.
Amen.**

The Blessing

The minister says the Grace or a suitable blessing.

Laying on of Hands
with Prayer and Anointing

*This form may be used at the prayers during the visitation of the sick,
either at Holy Communion with the sick or as part of another form of
prayer at the bedside. If Anointing is administered, the minister must be
authorized for this ministry as required by Canon B 37.*

Blessed are you, sovereign God, gentle and merciful.
Your anointed Son brought healing to those in weakness
    and distress;
he broke the power of evil and set us free from sin and death
that we might become partakers of his glory.
Remember in your mercy all for whom we pray;
in the fullness of time complete your gracious work
that we may be restored in your image, renewed in your love,
and for ever praise your great and holy name,
Father, Son and Holy Spirit.

Holy God, in whom we live and move and have our being,
we make our prayer to you saying,
Lord, hear us.
Lord, graciously hear us.

Grant to [N and] all who seek you
the assurance of your presence, your power and your peace.
Lord, hear us.
Lord, graciously hear us.

Grant your healing grace to [N and] all who are sick,
that they may be made whole in body, mind and spirit.
Lord, hear us.
Lord, graciously hear us.

Grant to all who minister to the suffering
wisdom and skill, sympathy and patience.
Lord, hear us.
Lord, graciously hear us.

Sustain and support the anxious and fearful
and lift up all who are brought low.
Lord, hear us.
Lord, graciously hear us.

Hear us, Lord of life.
Heal us, and make us whole.

O Lord our God, accept the fervent prayers of your people;
in the multitude of your mercies look with compassion
upon us and all who turn to you for help;
for you are gracious, O lover of souls,
and to you we give glory, Father, Son, and Holy Spirit,
now and for ever.
Amen.

The Laying on of Hands is administered.

In the name of God and trusting in his might alone,
receive Christ's healing touch to make you whole.

May Christ bring you wholeness
of body, mind and spirit,
deliver you from every evil,
and give you his peace.
Amen.

These words are used when Anointing is administered

N, I anoint you in the name of God who gives you life.
Receive Christ's forgiveness, his healing and his love.

May the Father of our Lord Jesus Christ
grant you the riches of his grace,
his wholeness and his peace.
Amen.

The minister says

The almighty Lord,
who is a strong tower for all who put their trust in him,
whom all things in heaven, on earth and under the earth obey,
be now and evermore your defence.
May you believe and trust that the only name under heaven
given for health and salvation
is the name of our Lord Jesus Christ.
Amen.

Emergency Baptism

For Notes, see page 48.

The following form is sufficient.

The minister pours water on the person to be baptized, saying

N, I baptize you in the name of the Father, and of the Son,
and of the Holy Spirit.

All **Amen.**

The minister may then say the Lord's Prayer and the Grace or a blessing.

If it is appropriate, some of the following may also be used.

Before the Baptism

Jesus says: I have come that you may have life
and have it in all its fullness.   *John 10.10*

All that the Father gives me will come to me;
and whoever comes to me I will not turn away.   *John 6.37*

The Lord is near to the brokenhearted
and will save those who are crushed in spirit.   *Psalm 34.18*

Heavenly Father,
grant that by your Holy Spirit
this child may be born again
and know your love in the new creation
given us in Jesus Christ our Lord.

All **Amen.**

At the Signing with the Cross

N, may Christ protect and defend you.
Receive the sign of his cross.

Prayer over the Water

Heavenly Father,
bless this water,
that whoever is washed in it
may be made one with Christ
in the fellowship of your Church,
and be brought through every tribulation
to share the risen life
that is ours in Jesus Christ our Lord.

All **Amen.**

As our Saviour taught us, so we pray

All   **Our Father in heaven,
hallowed be your name,
your kingdom come,
your will be done,
on earth as in heaven.
Give us today our daily bread.
Forgive us our sins
as we forgive those who sin against us.
Lead us not into temptation
but deliver us from evil.
For the kingdom, the power,
and the glory are yours
now and for ever.
Amen.**

(or)

Let us pray with confidence as our Saviour has taught us

All   **Our Father, who art in heaven,
hallowed be thy name;
thy kingdom come;
thy will be done;
on earth as it is in heaven.
Give us this day our daily bread.
And forgive us our trespasses,
as we forgive those who trespass against us.
And lead us not into temptation;
but deliver us from evil.
For thine is the kingdom,
the power and the glory,
for ever and ever.
Amen.**

Eternal God, our beginning and our end,
preserve in your people the new life of baptism;
as Christ receives us on earth,
so may he guide us through the trials of this world,
and enfold us in the joy of heaven,
where you live and reign,
one God for ever and ever.

All **Amen.**

The grace of our Lord Jesus Christ,
and the love of God,
and the fellowship of the Holy Spirit
be with us all evermore.

All **Amen.**

(or)

May God almighty,
the Father, the Son, and the Holy Spirit,
bless and keep you this day and for evermore.

All **Amen.**

1   In an emergency, a lay person may be the minister of baptism, and should subsequently inform those who have the pastoral responsibility for the person so baptized.

2   Parents are responsible for requesting emergency baptism for an infant. They should be assured that questions of ultimate salvation or of the provision of a Christian funeral for an infant who dies do not depend upon whether or not the child has been baptized.

3   Before baptizing, the minister should ask the name of the person to be baptized. When, through the absence of parents or for some other reason, there is uncertainty as to the name of the person, the baptism can be properly administered without a name (so long as the identity of the person baptized can be duly recorded).

Service in Church

4   If the person lives, they shall afterwards come to church, or be brought to church, and the service for Holy Baptism followed, except that the Signing with the Cross, the Prayer over the Water and the Baptism are omitted.

5   It may be appropriate to use the prayer of thanksgiving for a child from *Common Worship: Initiation Services* or the President's edition of *Common Worship*.

6   At the Presentation the president says

> We welcome *N,* who has been baptized and now comes to take *his/her* place in the company of God's people.

7   Oil mixed with fragrant spices (traditionally called chrism), expressing the blessings of the messianic era and the richness of the Holy Spirit, may be used to accompany the prayer after the baptism. It is appropriate that the oil should have been consecrated by the bishop.

Ministry at the Time of Death

¶ Preparation

¶ Reconciliation

¶ Opening Prayer

¶ The Word of God

¶ Prayers

¶ Laying on of Hands and Anointing

¶ Holy Communion

¶ Commendation

¶ Prayer when someone has just died

For Notes, see pages 50 and 69.

Ministry at the Time of Death

Note

Where possible the minister prepares the dying person in private,
using the Preparation and Reconciliation sections. The person
should be helped to be aware that the time of death is approaching.
Family and friends should join the minister and the dying person
at the Opening Prayer if they can be present, and it is appropriate
that they should receive Holy Communion with the dying person.
The different sections of the service may happen at different times,
and the last communion may be received on another occasion,
and more than once, as pastoral necessity dictates.

See further Notes on page 69.

¶ *Preparation*

*One or more of the following short texts may be said with the
dying person. They may be softly repeated two or three times.*

Who will separate us from the love of Christ?   *Romans 8.35*

Whether we live or whether we die, we are the Lord's.   *Romans 14.8*

Christ died and lived again, so that he might be Lord
of both the dead and the living.   *Romans 14.9*

We know that we have a building from God, a house
not made with hands, eternal in the heavens.   *2 Corinthians 5.1*

We will be with the Lord for ever.   *1 Thessalonians 4.17*

We will see God as he is.   *1 John 3.2*

To you, O Lord, I lift up my soul.   *Psalm 25.1*

The Lord is my light and my salvation; whom then shall I fear?

Psalm 27.1

I believe that I shall see the goodness of the Lord
in the land of the living.
Wait for the Lord;
be strong and he shall comfort your heart;
wait patiently for the Lord.   *Psalm 27.13,14*

Into your hands I commend my spirit;
for you have redeemed me, O Lord God of truth.   *Psalm 31.5*

My soul is athirst for God, even for the living God.   *Psalm 42.2*

Come, you that are blessed by my Father,
inherit the kingdom prepared for you
from the foundation of the world.   *Matthew 25.34*

The Lord Jesus says,
'Today you will be with me in Paradise.'   *Luke 23.43*

This is indeed the will of my Father,
that all who see the Son and believe in him
may have eternal life;
and I will raise them up on the last day.   *John 6.40*

In my Father's house there are many dwelling places.   *John 14.2*

I go and prepare a place for you.
And I will come again and will take you to myself,
so that where I am, there you may be also.   *John 14.3*

'I desire that those also, whom you have given me,
may be with me where I am, to see my glory,'
says the Lord Jesus.   *John 17.24*

Lord Jesus, receive my spirit.   *Acts 7.59*

The steadfast love of the Lord never ceases,
his mercies never come to an end;
they are new every morning;
great is your faithfulness.   *Lamentations 3.22,23*

The Lord's Prayer

As our Saviour taught us, so we pray

Our Father in heaven,
hallowed be your name,
your kingdom come,
your will be done,
on earth as in heaven.
Give us today our daily bread.
Forgive us our sins
as we forgive those who sin against us.
Lead us not into temptation
but deliver us from evil.
For the kingdom, the power,
and the glory are yours
now and for ever.
Amen.

(or)

Let us pray with confidence as our Saviour has taught us

Our Father, who art in heaven,
hallowed be thy name;
thy kingdom come;
thy will be done;
on earth as it is in heaven.
Give us this day our daily bread.
And forgive us our trespasses,
as we forgive those who trespass against us.
And lead us not into temptation;
but deliver us from evil.
For thine is the kingdom,
the power and the glory,
for ever and ever.
Amen.

Lord Jesus Christ,
Son of God,
have mercy on me,
a sinner.

(or)

Almighty God, our heavenly Father,
we have sinned against you,
through our own fault,
in thought and word and deed,
and in what we have left undone.
We are heartily sorry,
and repent of all our sins.
For your Son our Lord Jesus Christ's sake,
forgive us all that is past;
and grant that we may serve you in newness of life
to the glory of your name.
Amen.

(or)

Lord, have mercy upon us.
Christ, have mercy upon us.
Lord, have mercy upon us.

The minister may lay hands on the dying person.
If the minister is a priest, either of these absolutions may be used

God, the Father of mercies,
has reconciled the world to himself
  through the death and resurrection of his Son, Jesus Christ,
not counting our trespasses against us,
but sending his Holy Spirit to shed abroad his love among us.
By the ministry of reconciliation
entrusted by Christ to his Church,
receive his pardon and peace
to stand before him in his strength alone,
this day and evermore.
Amen.

If the minister is a deacon or lay person, these words are used

May almighty God have mercy on you,
forgive you your sins,
and bring you to everlasting life.
Amen.

At this point others may join the minister and the dying person.

¶ *Opening Prayer*

Blessed be the God and Father of our Lord Jesus Christ.
By his great mercy we have been born anew to a living hope
through the resurrection of Jesus Christ from the dead.

[*All*   **Blessed be God for ever.**]

Let us pray for …

(Silence)

This prayer may be used

Eternal God,
grant to your servant
[and to us who surround *him/her* with our prayers]
your peace beyond understanding.
Give us faith, the comfort of your presence,
and the words to say to one another and to you,
as we gather in the name of Jesus Christ our Lord.

All   **Amen.**

The following may be used

Out of the depths I cry to you:
Lord, hear my voice.
Lord, have mercy.

[*All*   **Lord, have mercy.**]

If you should mark what is done amiss:
who may abide it?
Christ, have mercy.

[*All*   **Christ, have mercy.**]

Trust in the Lord, for with him there is mercy:
for with him is ample redemption.
Lord, have mercy.

[*All*   **Lord, have mercy.**]

These or other suitable readings may be used (see pages 70–73 in this booklet and 383–391 in Common Worship: Pastoral Services)

Romans 8.35,37-39
Psalms 23; 139
John 6.35-40[53-58]

The minister may encourage an act of faith or commitment, such as

Holy God,
Father, Son, and Holy Spirit,
I trust you,
I believe in you,
I love you.

(or)

Jesus, remember me when you come into your kingdom.

(or)

Lord, I believe: help my unbelief.

(or)

Father, into your hands I commend my spirit.

¶ *Prayers*

This litany or some of the prayers with dying people on pages 74–75
may be used, or the minister may pray using his or her own words

God the Father,

All **have mercy upon us.**

God the Son,

All **have mercy upon us.**

God the Holy Spirit,

All **have mercy upon us.**

Holy, blessed and glorious Trinity,

All **have mercy upon us.**

By your holy incarnation, by your cross and passion,
by your precious death and burial,

All **have mercy upon us.**

By your glorious resurrection and ascension,
and by the coming of the Holy Spirit,

All **have mercy upon us.**

Graciously hear us, Lord Jesus Christ,
that it may please you to deliver your servant *N* from all evil
    and from eternal death,

All **hear us, good Lord.**

That it may please you mercifully to pardon all *N*'s sins,

All **hear us, good Lord.**

That it may please you to give *N* peace, rest and gladness,
raising *him/her* to new life in your kingdom,

All **hear us, good Lord.**

That it may please you to bring us, with *N* and all your saints,
to a joyful resurrection,

All **hear us, good Lord.**

Lamb of God, you take away the sin of the world,

All **hear us, good Lord.**

Lamb of God, you take away the sin of the world,

All **hear us, good Lord.**

Lamb of God, you take away the sin of the world,

All **hear us, good Lord.**

All **In darkness and in light,**
in trouble and in joy,
help us, O God, to trust your love,
to seek your purpose
and to praise your name;
through Jesus Christ our Lord.
Amen.

*The minister, together with others if that is appropriate,
may lay hands on the dying person. This prayer may be used*

In the name of our Lord Jesus Christ
I/we lay *my/our* hands on you, N.
May the Lord in his mercy and love uphold you
by the grace and power of the Holy Spirit.
May he deliver you from all evil,
give you light and peace,
and bring you to everlasting life.

All **Amen.**

*The minister may anoint the dying person, making the sign of the cross
in oil on his or her forehead [and hands] (see Note 1 on page 69)*

N, I anoint you with oil in the name of our Lord Jesus Christ.
May the Lord in his love and mercy uphold you
by the grace and power of the Holy Spirit.

All **Amen.**

When the anointing is completed, the minister may add

As you are outwardly anointed with this holy oil,
so may our heavenly Father grant you the inward anointing
    of the Holy Spirit.
Of his great mercy
may he forgive you your sins
and release you from suffering.
May he deliver you from all evil,
preserve you in all goodness
and bring you to everlasting life;
through Jesus Christ our Lord.

All **Amen.**

The Agnus Dei may be used before the giving of communion

Lamb of God,
you take away the sin of the world,
have mercy on us.

Lamb of God,
you take away the sin of the world,
have mercy on us.

Lamb of God,
you take away the sin of the world,
grant us peace.

(or)

Jesus, Lamb of God,
have mercy on us.

Jesus, bearer of our sins,
have mercy on us.

Jesus, redeemer of the world,
grant us peace.

After the words of distribution the following may be added

May the Lord Jesus protect you
and lead you to eternal life.

The Lord's Prayer

As our Saviour taught us, so we pray

All **Our Father in heaven,
hallowed be your name,
your kingdom come,
your will be done,
on earth as in heaven.
Give us today our daily bread.
Forgive us our sins
as we forgive those who sin against us.
Lead us not into temptation
but deliver us from evil.
For the kingdom, the power,
and the glory are yours
now and for ever.
Amen.**

(or)

Let us pray with confidence as our Saviour has taught us

All **Our Father, who art in heaven,
hallowed be thy name;
thy kingdom come;
thy will be done;
on earth as it is in heaven.
Give us this day our daily bread.
And forgive us our trespasses,
as we forgive those who trespass against us.
And lead us not into temptation;
but deliver us from evil.
For thine is the kingdom,
the power and the glory,
for ever and ever.
Amen.**

N, go forth from this world:
in the love of God the Father who created you,
in the mercy of Jesus Christ who redeemed you,
in the power of the Holy Spirit who strengthens you.
May the heavenly host sustain you
and the company of heaven enfold you.
In communion with all the faithful,
may you dwell this day in peace.

All **Amen.**

(or)

N, go forth upon your journey from this world,
in the name of God the Father almighty who created you;
in the name of Jesus Christ who suffered death for you;
in the name of the Holy Spirit who strengthens you;
in communion with the blessed saints,
and aided by angels and archangels,
and all the armies of the heavenly host.
May your portion this day be in peace,
and your dwelling the heavenly Jerusalem.

All **Amen.**

(and/or)

Holy Lord, almighty and eternal God,
hear our prayers as we entrust to you N,
as you summon *him/her* out of this world.
Forgive *his/her* sins and failings
and grant *him/her* a haven of light, and peace.
Let *him/her* pass unharmed through the gates of death
to dwell with the blessed in light,
as you promised to Abraham and his children for ever.
Accept N into your safe keeping
and on the great day of judgement
raise *him/her* up with all the saints
to inherit your eternal kingdom.
We ask this through Christ our Lord.

All **Amen.**

Gracious God,
nothing in death or life,
nothing in the world as it is,
nothing in the world as it shall be,
nothing in all creation
can separate us from your love.
Jesus commended his spirit into your hands at his last hour.
Into those same hands we now commend your servant *N*,
that dying to the world and cleansed from sin,
death may be for *him/her* the gate to life
and to eternal fellowship with you;
through the same Jesus Christ our Lord.

All **Amen.**

(and/or)

Into your hands, O merciful Saviour,
we commend your servant *N*.
Acknowledge, we pray, a sheep of your own fold,
a lamb of your own flock,
a sinner of your own redeeming.
Enfold *him/her* in the arms of your mercy,
in the blessed rest of everlasting peace
and in the glorious company of the saints in light.

All **Amen.**

For a further prayer, see page 75.

1   Now, Lord, you let your servant go in peace: ♦
       your word has been fulfilled.

2   My own eyes have seen the salvation ♦
       which you have prepared in the sight of every people;

3   A light to reveal you to the nations ♦
       and the glory of your people Israel.   *Luke 2.29-32*

Glory to the Father and to the Son
and to the Holy Spirit;
as it was in the beginning is now
and shall be for ever.
All   **Amen.**

(or)

1   Lord, now lettest thou thy servant depart in peace :
       according to thy word.

2   For mine eyes have seen :
       thy salvation;

3   Which thou hast prepared :
       before the face of all people;

4   To be a light to lighten the Gentiles :
       and to be the glory of thy people Israel.   *Luke 2.29-32*

Glory be to the Father, and to the Son :
and to the Holy Ghost;
as it was in the beginning, is now, and ever shall be :
world without end.
All   **Amen.**

(and/or)

All   **Give rest, O Christ, to your servant with the saints:**
where sorrow and pain are no more,
neither sighing, but life everlasting.
You only are immortal, the creator and maker of all:
and we are mortal, formed from the dust of the earth,
and unto earth shall we return.
For so you ordained when you created me, saying:
'Dust you are and to dust you shall return.'
All of us go down to the dust,
yet weeping at the grave we make our song:
Alleluia, alleluia, alleluia.

All   **Give rest, O Christ, to your servant with the saints:**
where sorrow and pain are no more,
neither sighing, but life everlasting.

(and/or)

At or just after death

1   Jesus, like a mother you gather your people to you; ♦
you are gentle with us as a mother with her children.

2   Often you weep over our sins and our pride, ♦
tenderly you draw us from hatred and judgement.

3   You comfort us in sorrow and bind up our wounds, ♦
in sickness you nurse us, and with pure milk you feed us.

4   Jesus, by your dying we are born to new life; ♦
by your anguish and labour we come forth in joy.

5   Despair turns to hope through your sweet goodness; ♦
through your gentleness we find comfort in fear.

6   Your warmth gives life to the dead, ♦
your touch makes sinners righteous.

7   Lord Jesus, in your mercy heal us; ♦
in your love and tenderness remake us.

8   In your compassion bring grace and forgiveness, ♦
for the beauty of heaven may your love prepare us.

A Song of St Anselm

The minister uses one of these blessings

May the eternal God
bless and keep us,
guard our bodies,
save our souls
and bring us safe to the heavenly country,
our eternal home,
where Father, Son, and Holy Spirit reign,
one God for ever and ever.

All   **Amen.**

(or)

God grant you to share in the inheritance of his saints in glory;
and the blessing of God almighty,
the Father, the Son, and the Holy Spirit,
be upon you, and remain with you always.

All   **Amen.**

The minister, a family member or a friend may use some or all of these words

In this moment of sorrow the Lord is in our midst
and consoles us with his word:

No eye has seen, nor ear heard, nor the human heart conceived,
what God has prepared for those who love him.

Blessed are the sorrowful; they shall be comforted.

Into your hands, O Lord,
we humbly entrust our *brother/sister N.*
In this life you embraced *him/her* with your tender love,
and opened to *him/her* the gate of heaven.
The old order has passed away,
as you welcome *him/her* into paradise,
where there will be no sorrow, no weeping nor pain,
but the fullness of peace and joy
with your Son and the Holy Spirit for ever and ever.

All **Amen.**

Heavenly Father,
into whose hands Jesus Christ
commended his spirit at the last hour:
into those same hands we now commend your servant *N*,
that death may be for *him/her*
the gate to life and to eternal fellowship with you;
through Jesus Christ our Lord.

All **Amen.**

Remember, O Lord,
this your servant,
who has gone before us with the sign of faith
and now rests in the sleep of peace.
According to your promises,
grant to *him/her* and to all who rest in Christ,
refreshment, light and peace;
through the same Christ our Lord.

All **Amen.**

Most merciful God,
whose wisdom is beyond our understanding,
surround the family of *N* with your love,
that they may not be overwhelmed by their loss,
but have confidence in your goodness,
and strength to meet the days to come.
We ask this through Christ our Lord.

All **Amen.**

Notes to
Ministry at the Time of Death

1   Where the minister is not a bishop or priest

    ¶   anointing is omitted;

    ¶   Holy Communion may be given but not celebrated;

    ¶   the usual alterations are made at the blessing.

2   The laying on of hands may be done by more than one person.

3   Canon B 37 provides that the priest should use 'pure olive oil consecrated by the bishop of the diocese or otherwise by the priest'. If consecrated oil is not available, the priest may use this form:

> Lord, holy Father, giver of health and salvation,
> as your apostles anointed those who were sick and healed them,
> so continue the ministry of healing in your Church.
> Sanctify this oil, that those who are anointed with it
> may be freed from suffering and distress,
> find inward peace, and know the joy of your salvation,
> through your Son, our Saviour Jesus Christ.
> **Amen.**

4   Wherever possible, care should be taken to use versions of texts familiar to the dying person.

Bible Readings and Psalms for Use at the Time of Death

Romans 8.35,37-39

Who will separate us from the love of Christ? Will hardship, or
distress, or persecution, or famine, or nakedness, or peril, or sword?
No, in all these things we are more than conquerors through
him who loved us. For I am convinced that neither death, nor life,
nor angels, nor rulers, nor things present, nor things to come, nor
powers, nor height, nor depth, nor anything else in all creation,
will be able to separate us from the love of God in Christ Jesus
our Lord.

Psalm 23

1 The Lord is my shepherd; ♦
 therefore can I lack nothing.

2 He makes me lie down in green pastures ♦
 and leads me beside still waters.

3 He shall refresh my soul ♦
 and guide me in the paths of righteousness for his name's sake.

4 Though I walk through the valley of the shadow of death,
  I will fear no evil; ♦
 for you are with me;
  your rod and your staff, they comfort me.

5 You spread a table before me
  in the presence of those who trouble me; ♦
 you have anointed my head with oil
  and my cup shall be full.

6 Surely goodness and loving mercy shall follow me
  all the days of my life, ♦
 and I will dwell in the house of the Lord for ever.

1   O Lord, you have searched me out and known me; ♦
you know my sitting down and my rising up;
    you discern my thoughts from afar.

2   You mark out my journeys and my resting place ♦
and are acquainted with all my ways.

3   For there is not a word on my tongue, ♦
but you, O Lord, know it altogether.

4   You encompass me behind and before ♦
and lay your hand upon me.

5   Such knowledge is too wonderful for me, ♦
so high that I cannot attain it.

6   Where can I go then from your spirit? ♦
Or where can I flee from your presence?

7   If I climb up to heaven, you are there; ♦
if I make the grave my bed, you are there also.

8   If I take the wings of the morning ♦
and dwell in the uttermost parts of the sea,

9   Even there your hand shall lead me, ♦
your right hand hold me fast.

10   If I say, 'Surely the darkness will cover me ♦
and the light around me turn to night,'

11   Even darkness is no darkness with you;
    the night is as clear as the day; ♦
darkness and light to you are both alike.

12   For you yourself created my inmost parts; ♦
you knit me together in my mother's womb.

13   I thank you, for I am fearfully and wonderfully made; ♦
marvellous are your works, my soul knows well.

14   My frame was not hidden from you, ♦
when I was made in secret
    and woven in the depths of the earth.

15   Your eyes beheld my form, as yet unfinished; ♦
already in your book were all my members written,

16 As day by day they were fashioned ♦
    when as yet there was none of them.

17 How deep are your counsels to me, O God! ♦
    How great is the sum of them!

18 If I count them, they are more in number than the sand, ♦
    and at the end, I am still in your presence.

19 O that you would slay the wicked, O God, ♦
    that the bloodthirsty might depart from me!

20 They speak against you with wicked intent; ♦
    your enemies take up your name for evil.

21 Do I not oppose those, O Lord, who oppose you? ♦
    Do I not abhor those who rise up against you?

22 I hate them with a perfect hatred; ♦
    they have become my own enemies also.

23 Search me out, O God, and know my heart; ♦
    try me and examine my thoughts.

24 See if there is any way of wickedness in me ♦
    and lead me in the way everlasting.

Jesus said to them, 'I am the bread of life. Whoever comes to me will never be hungry, and whoever believes in me will never be thirsty. But I said to you that you have seen me and yet do not believe. Everything that the Father gives me will come to me, and anyone who comes to me I will never drive away; for I have come down from heaven, not to do my own will, but the will of him who sent me. And this is the will of him who sent me, that I should lose nothing of all that he has given me, but raise it up on the last day. This is indeed the will of my Father, that all who see the Son and believe in him may have eternal life; and I will raise them up on the last day.'

[Jesus said to them, 'Very truly, I tell you, unless you eat the flesh of the Son of Man and drink his blood, you have no life in you. Those who eat my flesh and drink my blood have eternal life, and I will raise them up on the last day; for my flesh is true food and my blood is true drink. Those who eat my flesh and drink my blood abide in me, and I in them. Just as the living Father sent me, and I live because of the Father, so whoever eats me will live because of me. This is the bread that came down from heaven, not like that which your ancestors ate, and they died. But the one who eats this bread will live for ever.']

Additional Prayers with Dying People

1   Soul of Christ, sanctify me.
Body of Christ, save me.
Blood of Christ, refresh me.
Water from the side of Christ, wash me.
Passion of Christ, strengthen me.
O good Jesus, hear me.
Within your wounds hide me.
Let me never be separated from you.
From the power of darkness defend me.
In the hour of my death, call me
and bid me come to you,
that with your saints I may praise you
for ever and ever.
Amen.

2   Christ be with me, Christ within me,
Christ behind me, Christ before me,
Christ beside me, Christ to win me,
Christ to comfort and restore me,
Christ beneath me, Christ above me,
Christ in quiet, Christ in danger,
Christ in hearts of all that love me,
Christ in mouth of friend and stranger.

3   Lord Jesus Christ, we thank you
for all the benefits you have won for us,
for all the pains and insults you have borne for us.
Most merciful redeemer,
friend and brother,
may we know you more clearly,
love you more dearly,
and follow you more nearly,
day by day.
Amen.

4   Lord,
     in weakness or in strength
     we bear your image.
     We pray for those we love
     who now live in a land of shadows,
     where the light of memory is dimmed,
     where the familiar lies unknown,
     where the beloved become as strangers.
     Hold them in your everlasting arms,
     and grant to those who care
          a strength to serve,
          a patience to persevere,
          a love to last
          and a peace that passes human understanding.
     Hold us in your everlasting arms,
     today and for all eternity;
     through Jesus Christ our Lord.
     Amen.

At the time of death

Into your hands, Lord,
our faithful creator and most loving redeemer,
we commend your child *N*,
for *he/she* is yours in death as in life.
In your great mercy
fulfil in *him/her* the purpose of your love;
gather *him/her* to yourself in gentleness and peace,
that, rejoicing in the light and refreshment of your presence,
he/she may enjoy that rest which you have prepared
     for your faithful servants;
through Jesus Christ our Lord.

All   **Amen.**

Prayers for Protection and Peace

Notes

1. The following material may be used where it would be pastorally helpful to pray with those suffering from a sense of disturbance or unrest.

2. These pastoral prayers may be used by any minister as appropriate. The ministry of exorcism and deliverance may only be exercised by priests authorized by the bishop, who normally requires that permission be obtained from him for each specific exercise of such a ministry.

3. On occasions when exorcism and deliverance are administered, it is for the bishop to determine the nature of the rite and what form of words should be used.

Prayers for Protection and Peace

For a person or persons

May the Lord hear you in the day of trouble,
the name of the God of Jacob defend you;

Send you help from his sanctuary
and strengthen you out of Zion;

Remember all your offerings
and accept your burnt sacrifice;

Grant you your heart's desire
and fulfil all your mind.   *Psalm 20.1-4*
Amen.

Our Lord Jesus Christ,
present with us now in his risen power,
enter into your body and spirit,
take from you all that harms and hinders you,
and fill you with his healing and his peace.
Amen.

Christ be with you: Christ within you;
Christ before you: Christ behind you;
Christ on your right: Christ on your left;
Christ above you: Christ beneath you;
Christ around you: now and ever.

Bind unto yourself the name,
the strong name of the Trinity;
by invocation of the same,
the Three in One and One in Three.
Of whom all nature hath creation,
Eternal Father, Spirit, Word:
praise the Lord of your salvation,
salvation is of Christ the Lord.
Amen.

Almighty God, heavenly Father,
breathe your Holy Spirit into the heart of this your servant N
and inspire *him/her* with love for goodness and truth.
May *he/she*, fearing only you, have no other fear;
knowing your compassion, be ever mindful of your love;
and serving you faithfully unto death, live eternally with you;
through Jesus Christ our Lord.
Amen.

For a place

Visit, Lord, we pray, this place
and drive far from it all the snares of the enemy.
Let your holy angels dwell here to keep us in peace,
and may your blessing be upon it evermore;
through Jesus Christ our Lord.
Amen.

Christaraksha – an Indian Prayer

This prayer may be used in any of the following forms

I *For a person before sleep*
May the cross of the Son of God,
which is mightier than all the hosts of Satan
and more glorious than all the hosts of heaven,
abide with you in your going out and in your coming in.
By day and by night, at morning and at evening,
at all times and in all places may it protect and defend you.
From the wrath of evildoers, from the assaults of evil spirits,
from foes visible and invisible, from the snares of the devil,
from all passions that beguile the soul and body:
may it guard, protect and deliver you.
Amen.

(or)

May the risen and ascended Christ,
mightier than the hordes of hell,
more glorious than the heavenly hosts,
be with you in all your ways.
Amen.

May the cross of the Son of God
protect you by day and by night,
at morning and at evening,
at all times and in all places.
Amen.

May Christ Jesus guard and deliver you
from the snares of the devil,
from the assaults of evil spirits,
from the wrath of the wicked,
from all base passions
and from the fear of the known and unknown.
Amen.

And the blessing of God almighty,
the Father, the Son, and the Holy Spirit,
be upon you and remain with you always.
Amen.

(or)

3   *For individuals to say before sleep*

May the cross of the Son of God,
which is mightier than all the hosts of Satan,
and more glorious than all the hosts of heaven,
abide with me in my going out and my coming in.
By day and by night, at morning and at evening,
at all times and in all places may it protect and defend me.
From the wrath of evildoers, from the assaults of evil spirits,
from foes visible and invisible, from the snares of the devil,
from all passions that beguile the soul and body:
may it guard, protect and deliver me.
Amen.

Based on Psalm 91

Whoever dwells in the shelter of the Most High,
and abides under the shadow of the Almighty,

Shall say to the Lord, 'My refuge and my stronghold,
my God, in whom I put my trust.'

For he shall deliver you from the snare of the fowler
and from the deadly pestilence.

He shall cover you with his wings
    and you shall be safe under his feathers;
his faithfulness shall be my shield and buckler.

You shall not be afraid of any terror by night,
nor of the arrow that flies by day;

Of the pestilence that stalks in darkness,
nor of the sickness that destroys at noonday.

Because you have made the Lord your refuge
and the Most High my stronghold,

There shall no evil happen to you,
neither shall any plague come near my tent.

For he shall give his angels charge over you,
to keep me in all my ways.

We lift up our eyes to the hills;
from where is our help to come?

Our help comes from the Lord,
the maker of heaven and earth.

He will not suffer your foot to stumble;
he who watches over you will not sleep.

Behold, he who keeps watch over Israel
shall neither slumber nor sleep.

The Lord himself watches over you;
the Lord is your shade at your right hand,

So that the sun shall not strike you by day,
neither the moon by night.

The Lord shall keep you from all evil;
it is he who shall keep your soul.

The Lord shall keep watch over your going out
and your coming in,
from this time forth for evermore.

Authorization

¶ The following services and other material in *Common Worship: Pastoral Services* are authorized pursuant to Canon B 2 of the Canons of the Church of England for use until further resolution of the General Synod:

¶ Ministry to the Sick
¶ Emergency Baptism
¶ Prayers for Protection and Peace

¶ Ministry at the Time of Death and Prayers with Dying People have been commended by the House of Bishops of the General Synod pursuant to Canon B 2 of the Canons of the Church of England and are published with the agreement of the House (authorized texts are, however, incorporated in some of these forms).

Under Canon B 4 it is open to each bishop to authorize, if he sees fit, the form of service to be used within his diocese. He may specify that the services shall be those commended by the House, or that a diocesan form of them shall be used. If the bishop gives no directions in this matter the priest remains free, subject to the terms of Canon B 5, to make use of the services as commended by the House.

Acknowledgements

The publisher gratefully acknowledges permission to reproduce copyright material in this book. Every effort has been made to trace and contact copyright holders. If there are any inadvertent omissions we apologize to those concerned and undertake to include suitable acknowledgements in all future editions.

Published sources include the following:

The Archbishops' Council of the Church of England: *The Alternative Service Book 1980*; which is copyright © The Archbishops' Council of the Church of England.

Cambridge University Press: Extracts (and adapted extracts) from *The Book of Common Prayer*, the rights in which are vested in the Crown, are reproduced by permission of the Crown's Patentee, Cambridge University Press.

The Division of Christian Education of the National Council of Churches in the USA: Unless otherwise stated, Scripture quotations are from *The New Revised Standard Version of the Bible,* copyright © 1989 by the Division of Christian Education of the National Council of Churches in the USA. Used by permission. All rights reserved.

Thanks are also due to the following for permission to reproduce copyright material:

The Anglican Church in Aotearoa, New Zealand and Polynesia: (p. 62), prayer at the time of death ('N, go forth from this world: in the love of God the Father …'; Taken/adapted from *A New Zealand Prayer Book – He Karikia Mihinare O Aotearoa*, copyright © The Church of the Province of New Zealand 1989.

The Episcopal Church in the USA: 'Into your hands, O merciful Saviour …' (p. 63) from *The Book of Common Prayer* according to the use of the Episcopal Church of the USA, 1979. The ECUSA Prayer Book is not subject to copyright.